AVEBURY

Sun, Moon and Earth Energies

Maria Wheatley

Busty Taylor

First published in 2008 under the title:
'Avebury, Sun, Moon and Earth'. Reprinted 2009, 2011.
Published by Wessex Books, Salisbury, Wiltshire.

Second edition 2014 with additional material
by Maria Wheatley: Chapter 3.

Published by Celestial Songs Press,
Cherry Orchard, Marlborough,
Wiltshire. SN8 4AF.

www.theaveburyexperience.co.uk
Email: mariawheatley@aol.com
Telephone 01672 511427.

A CIP record for this book is available
from the British Library.

ISBN 978-0-9560733-5-8

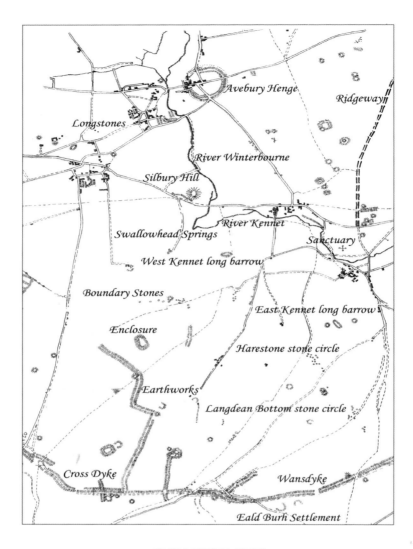

CONTENTS

ɞ

A *new view* of Avebury

For thousands of years Avebury's landscape has been seen as a mysterious region. The land has a peculiar sanctity and mystical power that has attracted people for millennia. Around five thousand years ago, some of the most complex and diverse monuments to be found in Britain were constructed in the Avebury area, which include the West Kennet long barrow, one of the most spectacular long barrows in the country, and Silbury Hill, the largest prehistoric mound in Europe. Avebury Henge is situated half a mile to the north of these sites and is the most impressive of all the stone circles in Britain. The sheer size of Avebury emphasises just how important this megalithic centre was to the prehistoric people who built it. Over the centuries, archaeologists and scholars have unearthed and discovered some of Avebury's history allowing us to understand the monument and to explore the ancient past. However, despite the archaeological excavations and numerous theories *something* important seemed to be missing and forgotten.

We discovered one of Avebury's best kept secrets. Within the stone temple there was once a spectacular astronomical alignment, which was closely associated with one of the most unusual megaliths in the entire complex, and we will explain why the stone was selected and also reveal its strange metaphysical properties.

Past and present theories are also explored which propose that Avebury's southern circle was dedicated to the sun and the northern circle was associated with the moon. Our photography has captured and confirmed several astronomical alignments, which show how Avebury's megalithic architects created an intimate relationship between the stone settings, the landscape and the rising and setting of heavenly bodies.

We also investigate the controversial subject of 'earth mysteries'. Avebury Henge is believed to be an ancient centre of power that incorporated ley lines and earth energies. Research over the past 80 years suggests that the location of important ancient sites was far from being an arbitrary choice. Site selection was due to the phenomenal earth energy patterns that were present and the megalithic architecture would be determined by the energy system, which as we shall see, produced unusual geophysical activity.

Our research suggests that the prehistoric architects were acutely aware of the earth's whispering energies and subtle geometries, and they integrated them into the foundation plans of their monuments using a long lost technology. We present a new, breath taking vision of the Avebury temple and the esoteric knowledge of its architects.

Chapter 1

The sun and the stones

Walking around Avebury today it's hard to imagine the original layout and design of the monument and the site can appear confusing, as although a number of standing stones are in their original positions, many others are missing and some still lie recumbent. A road bisects the undulating earthwork and a small village stands within the heart of the enclosure. Trees and buildings obscure important astronomical sightlines, and yet despite centuries of intrusion, Avebury Henge is considered the most impressive stone circle in Europe and one of the greatest achievements of the New Stone Age. This is no exaggeration as Avebury is the largest stone circle in the world and is a staggering 427 metres (1401 feet) in diameter and covers an area of 11.5 ha (28 acres). The immense earthwork that surrounds the stone circles consists of a bank and ditch, known as a 'henge', which undoubtedly belongs to the late Neolithic period of the Stone Age, dating to around 3100-2500 BC (orthodox dates; however, the timeline may be as far back as the Mesolithic era). The bank was originally around 8.6 metres (18 feet high), an estimated 200,000 tons of chalk was prised out of the ground to construct it. Initially, due to the chalk found beneath the surface in the Wessex region, the bank would have appeared white amid the lush green countryside.

Today the ditch is generally 3.7 metres (12 feet) deep, but this is due to the effects of weathering, which caused the sides to collapse and fill the ditch with chalk rubble and other forms of silting. The ditch was three times its present depth and only about 9 metres (29 feet) wide and even today the scale of the earthwork is impressive with the bank standing some 4-6 metres (13-15 feet) high. Undoubtedly, the henge served a metaphysical purpose - separating the sacred enclosure from the profane outer regions.

Inside the earthwork stood a massive stone circle of around 100 standing stones, the largest in prehistory, which enclosed two smaller stone circles. The northern inner circle once consisted of around 27-30 standing stones and at the centre stood a gigantic three-stone feature called the 'Cove'. The southern inner circle contained 29-30 megaliths and a massive stone, standing 6.4 metres (21 feet) known as the 'Obelisk' once dominated its centre. Around the Obelisk may have stood a rectangle of smaller sarsens of which only the west side known as the 'Z' stones remain. The Ring Stone, now just a stump of a stone, stood outside the inner circle and its partner formed an entrance into the southern inner circle. The Ring Stone had a natural perforation at its top corner and archaeologists suspect that before the earthen bank was raised it stood as an outlier to the southern circle. The henge had four entrances; the southern and western entrances being serviced by two stone avenues. The West Kennet Stone Avenue coursed for one and a half miles to a small concentric stone circle on Overton Hill called the Sanctuary and the Beckhampton Avenue coursed to the west terminating at Fox Covert. It is likely that the other

Avebury Henge reconstructed

The earthen bank once appeared chalk white separating
the sacred enclosure from the profane outer regions.

The villagers of the 14th century saved much of Avebury
as they buried many of the stones. In the 1930s Keiller
unearthed and re-erected some of them.

two entrances also had stone avenues that were used as processional ways into and out of the monument.

Avebury stood unmolested for 3500 years and apart from the effects of weathering remained virtually intact until the early part of the 14th century. Around AD 1320 many of the standing stones were deliberately toppled and buried. Although it is not known why this happened the process saved part of the monument. This is because in the 18th and 19th centuries Avebury was virtually destroyed. The magnificent henge bank was mutilated and many megaliths were toppled and broken up for building material. Those that remained buried were spared.

In the 1930s the marmalade millionaire and archaeologist, Alexander Keiller, bought the land containing Avebury, Windmill Hill and the West Kennet Stone Avenue and began to restore Avebury Henge. Out of the estimated 800 stones only 52 were still visible and only 25 remained standing. Keiller re-erected many of the megaliths that were previously buried or toppled, and when a stone hole was discovered that originally contained a megalith, a concrete marker was erected to depict its position, but the World War II and poor health stopped him restoring the entire monument. Today we see the brilliant restoration work of Keiller and his colleagues.

Astronomical stone temples in Wessex

According to archaeologists, Avebury has no major astronomical alignments whereas Stonehenge, situated 24 km (18 miles) to the south on Salisbury Plain, is world-famous for its spectacular solar alignment at the Summer Solstice (June 21st). However, careful analysis by the archaeo-astronomer Clive Ruggles suggests that the main solar orientation at Stonehenge was to the midwinter sunset, and there is good reasoning for this, as the five gigantic trilithons that were erected in a horseshoe shape graduate in height towards the south west and the midwinter sunset. Stonehenge is a solstice temple dedicated to the midsummer and midwinter festivals.

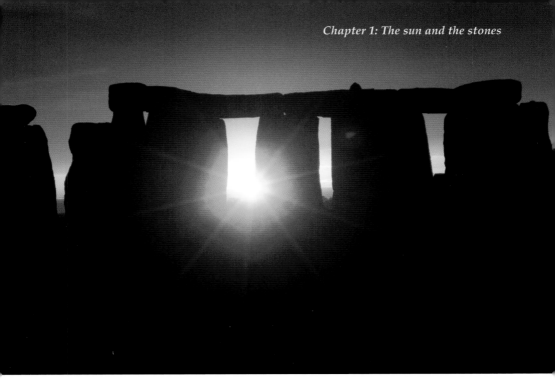

Midwinter sunset at Stonehenge

Throughout Great Britain and Europe numerous stone circles were designed to include stunning celestial alignments. Yet, despite being the largest stone circle in the world, Avebury is said to be devoid of any significant astronomical event. This simply isn't true. In 2005, we discovered a remarkable solar alignment at Avebury, which has gone by unnoticed for 4500 years, and incorporated one of the most unusual standing stones in the entire complex.

Avebury's lost alignment

The two gigantic southern portal stones create a grand entrance into the southern inner circle from the West Kennet Stone Avenue. The Devil's Chair (Stone no. 1) is a huge stone measuring 4.30 metres (14 feet) wide by 3.98 metres (13 feet) tall and weighs around 60 tons. This megalith has a curious ledge and numerous tourists have their photograph taken whilst sat on the stone ledge or 'chair'. Many theories have been put forward to explain why this standing stone has a seat. One claim suggests that it was used to enhance fertility in young women and even in the 20th century young girls on Beltane (May Day) would sit on the Devil's Chair and make wishes. No other standing stone at Avebury has such a strange feature. So why did the ancient architects erect this unusual megalith and for what purpose?

The Druid's Chair

The Outer Circle of around 100 standing stones, which includes the Devil's Chair, was erected around 2600 BC (orthodox dating) and the henge bank was also expanded and heightened during this phase, creating one of the largest henges ever constructed in Britain. However, the henge bank south of the Devil's Chair is no longer in its original position as it was lengthened around 200 years ago and today beech trees crown part of this 'false' bank. Initially, the bank and ditch was 11.30 metres (37 feet) further back creating a much wider entrance. Standing in front of the giant portal stones and either side of the causeway entrance were two standing stones that were once part of the West Kennet Stone Avenue, which was used as a processional way into Avebury's stone circles. A concrete plinth now marks the position of one of the avenue stones, known as *avenue stone 1a* and its partner *avenue stone 1b* is underneath the road. Taken back to its original design with the henge bank in the correct position, whilst sat on the Devil's Chair, a spectacular view of the rising midwinter sun would have been seen which explains the curious seat.

The Devil's Chair

Perhaps the Devil's Chair was reserved for an important priest or priestess who conducted the midwinter ceremony and who would have witnessed an extraordinary solstice event.

Four and a half thousand years ago, the rising midwinter sun would have been clearly visible through the causeway entrance, and as the sun rose higher and brighter, it would have been framed by the avenue stones 1a and 1b and

flooded the entrance with light. To prehistoric people the Winter Solstice was an important event as it marked a turning point in the year, when the seasonal flow turned from the darkness of winter towards longer and brighter days. The Church officially Christianised this popular pagan date during the 4th century AD, when Pope Julius I suggested December 25th marked the birth of Jesus. However, from time immemorial this ancient Solstice Day represented the rebirth of the sun, heralding new life and regeneration throughout the pagan world.

Midwinter sunset from the Devil's Chair

The angle and location of the Devil's Chair also allows a perfect view of the setting midwinter sun and you can still see part of this event today; although the full sunset is partly obstructed by a modern building. We recommend that you sit on the Devil's Chair and watch the setting sun and discover this esoteric alignment for yourself.

Gors Fawr's megalithic chair

The positioning of this megalith cannot be coincidental and we are convinced that the Devil's Chair was one of the most important megaliths at Avebury and its unique feature and subtle orientation reveals one of Avebury's forgotten alignments.

Although megalithic viewing-chairs are rare another example can be found in Wales. Idyllically situated close to the Preseli mountains in Pembrokeshire stands a small stone circle known as Gors Fawr, which is 22.3 metres (73 feet) in diameter and consists of 16 stones. Approximately 134 metres (440 feet) north east of the circle is a pair of standing stones set 14.6 metres (48 feet) apart which are aligned in a north eastern direction towards the midsummer sunrise and the midwinter sunset. The western stone is 1.9 metres (6 feet) high and the eastern megalith is 1.7 metres (5 feet 7 inches) in height, and its unusual shape forms a seat that allows a perfect view of the midwinter sunset.

Stone chair at Gors Fawr

Strange anomalies

Intriguingly, both viewing chairs emit unusual levels of magnetism and when used as seats certain areas of the body are affected by the stone's magnetic field. Earth mysteries writer and researcher, Paul Devereux, suggests that a shamanic priest who had induced an altered state of consciousness by meditation, fasting or 'hallucinogenics' may have used the stone chair at Gors Fawr for ritual purposes. Whilst sat on the chair the head, and thus the brain, leans directly upon a magnetic 'hot-spot', which could enhance spiritual visions and experiences, as magnetism can subtly affect consciousness by stimulating the temporal region of the brain, which is particularly sensitive to electromagnetic fields. We discovered that the Devil's Chair also has an active magnetic zone and

> *We discovered that the Devil's Chair has a strange magnetic hotspot. When sat in the chair your head touches the magnetic zone. The same phenomenon occurs at Gors Fawr.*

when sat on the stone ledge the neck and head areas of the body rest upon the magnetic hotspot. It is highly likely that both megaliths were deliberately selected because of their unique magnetic properties and distinctive shapes and erected as ceremonial stone chairs. We suspect that there are other megalithic viewing-chairs, perhaps recumbent and lying face down hiding their original purpose. In the 1940s the field archaeologist and Master Dowser, Guy Underwood, discovered an unusual viewing chair near Bath. He claimed that a stone circle had *its priest's seat still in place*. The megalith was carved complete with armrests and faced the midsummer sunrise. Sadly, it was destroyed by foresters in the 1950s.

Avebury Henge - a solar calendar

Several other solar alignments were skilfully integrated into Avebury's megalithic architecture creating a dynamic and sophisticated sundial calendar. The first to recognise this was Thomas Maurice. Writing in 1801 he suggested that the huge Obelisk Stone, the central megalith of Avebury's southern inner circle, could be used as a sundial stone to establish the time of the year. At the turn of the last century, Moses Cotsworth suggested that a 29-metre (95 feet) wooden pole placed on the summit of Silbury Hill would create exceptional shadow effects and that Silbury *was a gigantic sundial to determine the seasons and the true length of the year*. In the mid-90s, Dr. Terence Meaden, author of *The Secrets of the Avebury Stones*. Souvenir Press 1999 elaborated upon these theories and rediscovered Avebury's remarkable sundial system. Meaden calculated that at sunrise at specific times of the year the shadow of the Obelisk Stone would fall upon and align with a particular megalith within the southern inner circle. European photographer Jan Bily captured the remarkable sundial-effect at a stone circle in Portugal, and when Avebury's southern inner circle was in pristine condition and fully functional the visual effect would have been similar.

The sun and the pagan year

For some 10,000 years ever since men learned to grow and harvest crops their survival became dependant on the seasonal tides of the sun. The sun became the supreme deity throughout the ancient world representing life, light, growth, power and rebirth. It was vitally important to determine the agricultural year and the ancients achieved this by observing the sun's position in the heavens.

The sun marks the year at four distinct points called the Quarter Days - the Winter Solstice (shortest day and longest night), the Spring Equinox (equal day and night), the Summer Solstice (longest day and shortest night), and the Autumn Equinox (equal day and night). The Celts divided the year into eight by inserting the four Cross Quarter Days at roughly November 1st (Samhain), February 1st (Imbolc), May 1st (Beltane) and August 1st (Lughnasadh or Lammas). These points are roughly half the number of days between the Solstices and the Equinoxes. Samhain (Halloween) is the end and the beginning of the Old Celtic year. Representing a ceremonial cycle, the festival dates were celebrated throughout Old Europe and were eventually Christianised by the Church.

Celtic days and Avebury

Terence Meaden discovered that Avebury's southern circle formed an intimate relationship with the sun and the pagan year. At the eight festival dates the rising and setting sun activated the Obelisk Stone whose broad shadow would fall upon a single megalith, and like the hand of a clock the shadow would announce the exact time of the festival date. No doubt, elaborate ceremonies and rituals took place synchronising with this incredible visual event.

Terence Meaden's sundial calendar at Avebury

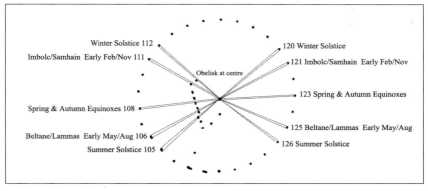

Stone numbers 105-112 are the sunrise stones and stones 120-126 are the sunset stones

Meaden's calculations which are shown in the illustration reveal how the sundial-shadow system functions. For example, at dawn on Summer Solstice (June 21st), the low angle of the rising sun would cause the shadow of the central Obelisk Stone to fall directly upon Stone 105 and at sunset the Obelisk's shadow would fall upon Stone 126. We carefully studied Meaden's findings and observed what was left of Avebury's sundial system and discovered that the Obelisk's shadow-effect, which targets a single standing stone is only a small part of the visual drama that was incorporated into the southern circle. We noticed that the overall shadow-effect produced by the setting sun is far more elaborate than previously thought. For example, Meaden calculated that as the sun sets at the Winter Solstice the shadow of the Obelisk would fall upon Stone 120. However, the megalithic shadow-sequence actually begins with the shadow of Stone 105 falling directly upon the Obelisk Stone whose dark shadow then touched Stone 120, creating a dark shadow-line around 100 metres (328 feet) long that stretched from one side of the southern circle to the other. Fortunately, our theory can be proved as you can still see the first part of the enigmatic shadow-line today. However, the position of a tall tree on the south west side of the outer circle interferes and weakens the strength of the sun, so that the shadow of Stone 105 can no longer touch the Obelisk Stone as once intended. If the tree was pruned, this section of the shadow-line would be exact and, either side of the shadow-line, shafts of bright sunlight would be visible.

The Winter Solstice shadow-line

We discovered that due to the architectural design of the monument the extended shadow-line can *only* occur at sunset on the festival dates. For instance, at sunrise on the early November festival of Samhain, the shadow of the Obelisk Stone would fall directly upon Stone 111, whereas at sunset the shadow of Stone 106 fell upon the Obelisk Stone, and its broad shadow then touched Stone 121. If the extended shadow-line was intended to be a visual design feature, why were the ancients emphasising the importance of the sunsets, and what is the significance of the gigantic shadow-line?

Today, the sunrise at dawn marks the start of a day, but to the Celts the day began at sunset, as recorded by Julius Caesar in his *Dis Pater* discussion in his *The Conquest of Gaul* (VI.18). It is from this Druid custom that we derive so many 'eve' festivals. Thus, in prehistoric times each pagan festival-day actually *began* in the evening and perhaps at Avebury the long shadow-line, which stretched across the diameter of the stone circle, symbolically announced the holy day and the commencement of ritual activity. We suggest that the geomantic architects achieved the vast shadow-line by altering the ground level upon which Avebury stands. The north-south axis line of Avebury and the centres of the northern and southern circles stand on elevated ground, whilst the ground level is significantly lower in the north-east,

Obelisk marker stone

Shadow of Stone No. 105

The shadow of Stone 105 once touched the Obelisk Stone creating the first section of the dramatic 100-metre (328 feet) Winter Solstice shadow-line

south-east, north-west and south-west sectors. By modifying the land level of the site and creating a sloping effect the length of a shadow at sunrise and sunset is maximised.

Avebury's southern circle contains one of the oldest solar calendars in the world and this system of timing invented in the Neolithic era was used for nearly 4000 years by rural folk. As late as the 19th century farmers used a similar method to fix the solstices: a stone was set in the earth from which solar observations were made that assisted the timing and planning of the approaching harvest. Before the invention of the medieval clock, the Christian church adopted this pagan system to time their holy vespers and services. 'Service-dials' are stones which work like primitive sundials and they can be found at old churches throughout Wiltshire. One of the best examples can be seen at Yatesbury church near Avebury as shown in the photograph on the following page. By placing a thin piece of wood into the central hole, the shadow cast upon the carved lines informed the church officials of forthcoming services.

Today, little is left of Avebury's megalithic sundial; however with perfect weather conditions you can see the first section of the extended sunset shadow-line at the Winter Solstice, and possibly at Imbolc (Early February) and Samhain (Early November). Whilst the southern circle featured striking solar alignments, the northern circle was closely associated with the moon. William Stukeley was the first to recognise Avebury's sun-moon relationship, and proposed that the southern circle was the *temple of the*

sun, whilst the northern circle was the *temple of the moon* and as we shall see, his intuitive insight was prophetic.

Lunar alignments

Dated to around 3000 BC (orthodox dating) the central Cove Stones stand at the heart of the northern circle. Originally the Cove consisted of three huge megaliths; a large diamond shaped 'feminine' stone, which is the heaviest megalith in Britain weighing around 100 tons, and two tall 'male' or 'phallic' stones. Today only two standing stones remain as one of the male stones was demolished in 1713.

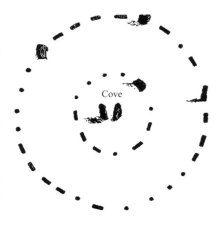

The Cove and the moon

The archaeologist, Aubrey Burl, suggested that the Cove Stones may have been aligned to the moon's northernmost moonrise which only occurs once every 18.61 years. In December 2006 we watched this rare lunar event and confirmed the alignment. When viewed from the Cove Stones the full moon gracefully rises over the horizon and is embraced by the stone setting, which created an intimate enclosure for ceremonies probably dedicated to the Neolithic moon goddess. Interestingly, the long axis of the tall 'male' stone aligns perfectly with the moonrise, which may explain the stones unusual angle and position. It is tempting to think that monthly full moon ceremonies were conducted from the Cove Stones, with a major festival occurring once every 18.61 years to coincide with the Cove's lunar alignment.

Temple of the moon

The northernmost moonrise viewed from the Cove Stones. The next major alignment will be in 2025

Solstice shadows at the Cove Stones

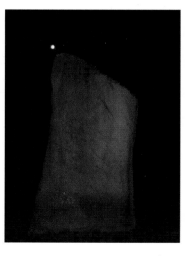

Around 2800 BC (orthodox dating) the inner stone circle of 27-30 standing stones was erected and the Cove became its central feature. Stukeley believed another circle consisting of 12 stones stood concentric with it as shown in the illustration opposite. Recent geophysical surveys suggest that a façade of smaller stones once flanked the front of the Cove and outlying stones may have stood at the north-east, south-east, north-west and south-west sectors. Terence Meaden argues that the Cove feature was dedicated to the Summer Solstice sunrise and a single shadow alignment.

Lunar alignments are far more exact than the Summer Solstice solar alignment

Meaden calculated that at dawn the midsummer sun would have risen directly behind a small megalith, known as 'Stone F', (possibly one of the 12 stones of the innermost concentric circle) and its shadow-line would have touched the lower part of the large diamond shaped Cove Stone. This unique event synchronised with the Obelisk's shadow-line touching Stone 105 in the adjacent southern circle, and if Terence Meaden's calculations are correct, the midsummer sunrise activated and united Avebury's stone circles, which visually announced the longest day of the year.

Throughout Britain astronomical alignments and shadow-lines were skilfully encoded into numerous ancient sites and one of the finest examples is Newgrange in Ireland. Dated to around 3200 BC (orthodox dating) Newgrange is a kidney shaped Neolithic chambered tomb, which covers an area of over one acre and is surrounded by 97 kerbstones, some of which are richly decorated with megalithic art.

The 19 metre (62 foot) long inner passage leads to a cruciform chamber with a corbelled roof. Newgrange is famous for its midwinter alignment when the passage and chamber are illuminated by the Winter Solstice sunrise. A shaft of sunlight shines through the deliberately designed roof box over the entrance and penetrates the passage to light up the chamber. The dramatic event lasts for around 17 minutes at dawn from the 19-23 of December. Newgrange also featured extraordinary shadow-lines which were discovered by Martin Brennan.

On important dates of the Celtic year, the outlying stones at Newgrange were positioned so that their shadow-lines would target the enigmatic rock carvings on the edging stones that surround the mound. The ancient artistry of constructing megalithic shadow-lines must have created a sense of geomantic wonder bestowed with esoteric and religious meaning. Some archaeologists suggest the design was an essential part of ancestral worship that was common throughout Europe during the Neolithic era. Whilst Meaden argues for ancient fertility rites at the eight festival dates when the dark 'phallic' shadow of the 'male' Obelisk Stone impregnated a 'feminine' diamond shaped stone that signified a divine cosmic-union. Yet, as we have seen the 'feminine' stones can also cast so-called 'phallic-like' shadows that can impregnate the 'male' Obelisk Stone, which casts some doubt upon this theory. Perhaps the shadows pointed to healing stones whose strength was believed to peak at the eight festival days, or did they simply announce the festival date. Although the real meaning is now lost, we can still visit these remarkable ancient sites and see for ourselves the stunning astronomical alignments and their unusual visual effects.

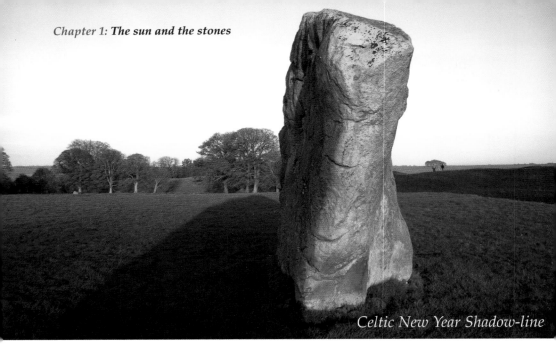

Celtic New Year Shadow-line

Witness a shadow-line at Avebury

During our investigations at Avebury we discovered an intriguing shadow-line that coincided with the Celtic New Year. Samhain (Early November festival) means the 'end of summer' and heralds the darkness of the coming winter. It was the start of the Old Druid year when the gods drew near to the earth, and when the veil to the Otherworld is the thinnest. At sunset the southern portal stones (Devil's Chair and Stone 98) cast a long black co-joined shadow, which stretches across the ground in front of the causeway entrance and terminates at the henge bank. To enter the southern inner circle one would have to walk across this dark shadow-line and we surmise that this was an esoteric design feature. Fortuitously, both megaliths are still in their original positions and you can see this archaic shadow-path today on the 4th-7th November, as the photograph above shows.

The shadow-path of Castlerigg

There is evidence to suggest that shadow-lines actually inspired the positioning of ancient sites. Situated among the mountains in the heart of the Lake District stands an enchanting stone circle called Castlerigg. Dated to around 3200 BC (orthodox dating) it could be one of the earliest stone circles in Europe. Researcher John Glover discovered that at the midsummer sunset the tallest stone in the ring casts an incredible shadow-line. He surveyed the line and found that it extended for approximately 3 km (2 miles) and that ancient sites were set along the axis. We have seen that a fundamental aspect of the Old Religion was to encode their stone temples with a solar alignment that produced a dramatic shadow effect. This ancient rite gave visual awareness of the intimate relationship between man, the heavenly sun and the ebb and flow of the ceremonial year. However, this is only one-step towards understanding sacred sites. To the prehistoric architects the location was equally as important as the monument and another essential design canon was to incorporate 'earth energies' into the foundation plans of their monuments, which gave the site magio-religious powers.

Round and round in circles...

Stone circles that have retained their circular shape, such as Castlerigg and Swinside stone circles in Cumbria; Beltany stone circle in Ireland, and the Rollright Ring in Oxfordshire, generate a distinctive form of dowseable aerial energy called 'form energy'.

All circular shapes generate form energy which casts concentric circles of energetic power within and without of the circle. Occultists understand the esoteric significance of the circle – and its protective and all-powerful form energy.

Chapter 2

Exploring earth mysteries

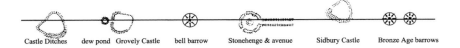

Castle Ditches   dew pond Grovely Castle   bell barrow   Stonehenge & avenue   Sidbury Castle   Bronze Age barrows

Dowsers claim that most ancient sites are located above powerful energy-lines and geometric earth energy patterns, which dictated the position and the shape of a prehistoric monument. Earth energies are said to personify sacred space and are believed to be magnetic lines of force, which psychic and sensitive people say they can sense or feel. We decided to explore the controversial subject of leys and earth energies and investigated Avebury's energy-lines and flows for their dowseable energies as well as measuring their magnetic and radiation anomalies.

Leys

Straight track ways and linear alignments are believed to connect sites of ancient importance to one another in a system that was designed in prehistoric times. In 1925 Alfred Watkins rediscovered the ancient ley network and published his seminal findings in a book called *The Old Straight Track*. He noticed that straight lines, sometimes old tracks and pathways, formed linear alignments across the countryside and that ancient manmade structures were sited upon them, such as tumuli, long barrows, stone circles, and standing stones. Watkins called these simple linear alignments 'leys'.

With the arrival of Earth Mysteries came controversial speculation that leys were once used to levitate gigantic stones across the landscape to construct megalith sites and some ley line enthusiasts have connected UFOs and paranormal events to the humble ley.

Researcher and writer Paul Devereux offers a more down-to-earth interpretation. He collected evidence from around the world to support the concept that leys had ritual significance and were created as 'spirit ways' and 'death roads'. After undergoing actual or symbolic death, the shaman's soul or astral body would travel along the dead straight line. Devereux noted that the Medieval Dutch 'Doodwegen', (death roads), ran in straight lines to cemeteries and likewise, the Vikings once used straight roads in their death ceremonies. Straight tracks coursed across Costa Rica and were used for similar purposes and old Germanic folklore states that 'Geisterwegen' (ghost paths) were thought to course invisibly and in straight lines between cemeteries. According to ancient Chinese lore, straight lines conduct 'sha chi' (negative energy) and should be avoided as spirits travel in straight routes along the ancestral pathways. Devereux raises some interesting ideas, but is there more to the ley than he suggests? Since the 1940s dowsers have reported finding 'energies' whilst investigating leys. Sig Lonegren, the well-known American dowser, recognised that there are different types of ley lines which he categorised.

The Topographical ley is the traditional Watkins' style of linear alignment and perhaps Devereux's 'spirit line'.

The Energy ley appears to transmit energy, or follow invisible lines of power and this subtle energy can be detected using a dowsing instrument. Ancient man may have been aware of this natural power and harnessed it by constructing monuments upon the energy lines.

The Astronomical ley are leys that were orientated towards the sun or a celestial object and this is supported by the fact that numerous ancient roads and straight tracks follow the course of the sun at ceremonial times of the year. During the 1920s, the archaeo-astronomer, Admiral Boyle Somerville, compiled a study of ley alignments in Scotland and Ireland. He noted that several leys would course from a stone row, circle or dolmen to a barrow on a hill summit several miles away.

*The Belinus and the
St Michael leys*

Belinus Line

Michael Line

Many of these leys were orientated to one of the Celtic
festival dates. For instance, in Co. Donegal, Ireland, a ley was
orientated to the Beltane (Early May) sunrise that connected
a stone circle on Beltany Hill to a barrow on a hill summit
several miles away. The illustration above shows two of the
longest leys in Britain. The well-documented St. Michael ley
courses west-east from Carn Les Boel in Cornwall, to Hopton
in Norfolk and was orientated to the rising Beltane sun and
the setting Samhain (Early November) sun. The Belinus line
investigated by Gary Biltcliffe and Caroline Hoare courses
from the Isle of Wight to Inverhope in Scotland and was

aligned to the midday sun at the Summer Solstice and, intriguingly, many times in our history the Belinus line has fallen exactly on magnetic north. These three main types of ley lines are apparent throughout the ancient world and although the original purpose of the ley has long been forgotten, it is evident that prehistoric people created a vast network of linear lines that shaped the ancestral landscape.

As we shall soon see, the positioning of prehistoric sites was not confined to ley lines. Dragon lines coil around a ley in a caduceus-like fashion and meander across the landscape like mighty rivers of invisible energy. They flow relatively close to one another as they twist and coil around the ley.

We consider that the ley anchors and controls the two yin yang currents that entwine it and this ancient geomantic practice was known throughout the ancient world.

Dragon lines

According to ancient philosophy there are two powerful currents of earth energy that run invisibly over the entire planet. The Chinese Feng Shui Masters referred to these energies as 'lung mei' the 'dragon's breath'. One current is considered male (yang energy) and the other current is considered female (yin energy) and collectively they are referred to as 'dragon lines'. In Old China buildings would be aligned along the dragon lines to achieve a harmonious and natural rapport with the earth. Where the dragon lines crossed represented a place of special sanctity and would be reserved for the sites of temples or the tombs of emperors. The ancient Chinese philosophy of Feng Shui is generally described as geomancy or earth magic and the Chinese regard it as a perfect amalgamation of religion and science. Its origin can be traced to remote ages and it has a deep respect and reverence for the spirit and power of Nature. Feng Shui teaches that the earth is sacred and that any alterations to, or building on it, must be in accordance with Divine Laws and in such a way as not to interrupt or disturb the yin and yang dragon lines. In the nineteenth century, when a road was cut to the Happy Valley in Hong Kong, the Chinese community were thrown into abject terror, as the foreign construction company had amputated a dragon line, which the Chinese said would bring disaster. When many engineers employed at the site died of fever and the foreign houses built in Happy Valley had to be deserted on account of sudden outbreaks of malaria, the Chinese triumphantly declared that it was an act of retributive justice by Feng Shui. Topographical features of the Chinese landscape were deliberately altered; a pointed hill summit would be made round, and river courses were changed, so that the dragon current would flow harmoniously across the countryside, bringing peace and prosperity to the land and its people.

The dragon and the ley

The knowledge of dragon lines was not confined to ancient China, but known globally as numerous sacred sites throughout the world were sited upon dragon lines. For reasons unknown, dowsing experts have noticed that certain ley and dragon lines are intimately associated, as the yin/yang currents coil around the ley.

The positioning of prehistoric sites was not confined to ley lines. The ancient priesthood recognised that there was a natural omnipresent energy within the land that was regarded as supernatural and divine. Although invisible, its presence was marked by sacred sites, creating holy places where the powerful energies of the Earth are ever present.

The living Earth Force breathes life into a monument and bestows it with unseen energy that is beneficial to all life forms.

Straight lines conduct 'sha chi' or inharmonious energy as energy travels too fast along a linear line. This is why the roofs of traditional Chinese houses are never straight but gently curve to form a 'U' shape.

The horseshoe shape generates a harmonious energy conducive to good health, wealth and longevity.

Feng Shui at Avebury

In the 1980s the late Hamish Miller and Paul Broadhurst rediscovered the British yin/yang dragon lines Mary and Michael, which are associated with the St. Michael ley. The Mary and Michael dragon lines target numerous sacred sites, such as St. Michael's Mount in Cornwall, Glastonbury Tor, in Somerset and Hopton on the Norfolk coast in their sinuous journey across the landscape. In the Avebury region, the Mary and Michael dragon lines are associated with all the important Neolithic and Bronze Age sites, such as the Sanctuary, Avebury Henge, Windmill Hill's causewayed enclosure, the West Kennet long barrow and Silbury Hill.

Following the path of the dragon

The Michael current enters the Avebury region from the west and flows across the ancient earthworks on Knoll Down. It then crosses the main road and follows an old lane that marks the precise width of the current, and enters the Neolithic causeway enclosure on Windmill Hill where it targets a large bell barrow upon the summit. The male current then flows downhill following another ancient track and enters the Henge from the north and passes through the Cove Stones and then targets the Obelisk marker stone in the southern circle. The current passes through the southern causeway entrance and on to the West Kennet Stone Avenue, where the megaliths set the exact width of the Michael earth current, which visually defines its presence in the ritual landscape and then on to the Sanctuary's centre.

Mary's graceful route

Mary passes through the bubbling waters of the Swallowhead Springs, and then targets a Neolithic long barrow near the Beckhampton road. She then heads for two standing stones called the 'Longstones', known locally as 'Adam' and 'Eve', which are the sole survivors of the Beckhampton Stone

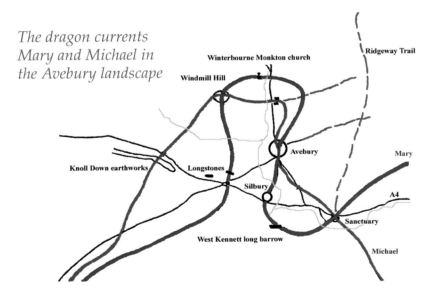

The dragon currents Mary and Michael in the Avebury landscape

Avenue and Cove feature. Mary then flows uphill and crosses with Michael at the bell barrow upon Windmill Hill, and passes through the Winterbourne Monkton church, setting its axis and its width. The female current then curves around to the north of Avebury and enters the henge and targets one of the few surviving megaliths (Stone 201) of the northern circle and on to the 'Cove' feature. Here she flows conjointly with Michael through the Obelisk marker stone and the southern portal stones where she departs on her own to target Silbury Hill, the West Kennet long barrow, and finally crosses with Michael at the Sanctuary. Here we see Neolithic Feng Shui practised on a magnificent scale.

The Great north-south line

Gary Biltcliffe and Caroline Hoare discovered that the Belinus ley also has two dragon lines associated with it called 'Elen' and 'Belinus', which frequently target numerous ancient sites in England and Scotland. Mirroring the geomantic integration of the Dragon currents in the Avebury environs, Gary and Caroline discovered that Elen and Belinus are connected with all the prehistoric sites in the nearby Uffington complex, which is situated 24 km (18 miles) north east of Avebury.

Caroline noted that in the nearby Uffington church, the two mighty female dragon currents Mary and Elen did not interact with one another. Interestingly, Elen crosses over the Mary current beneath the tower.

Detecting the dragon's power

To the sceptic the existence of dragon lines is purely anecdotal and there is no hard evidence to confirm their presence in the landscape. Energy lines documented by the ancient Chinese could be interpreted as legendary tales and verification of the British dragon lines originated from dowsers such as Hamish Miller and Gary Biltcliffe. They claim dowsing instruments can detect the subterranean flow and believe that the lines are electromagnetic currents of invisible energy - although this theory has never been proved. Do these underground currents really exist or are they simply a figment of the dowser's imagination? As a second-generation dowser I *know* that dowsing works and I can detect earth and ley energies, however, I wanted to prove to sceptics, by gathering solid and compelling evidence for unseen energies within the earth. Believing is not enough.

We consulted Rodney Hale an expert in measuring, recording and analysing electromagnetic frequencies to join us at Avebury to investigate the Mary and Michael earth currents. If the earth energies are electromagnetic the emitted frequency level could be detected and recorded which would prove their existence. If on the other hand no electromagnetic signals were present then dragon lines cannot be associated with magnetism and another New Age myth would be disproved.

Using sensitive electronic equipment an area just south of the Obelisk marker stone was chosen as the dragon lines flow co-terminously at this location. Rodney used two electronic copper based probes that were set in the ground 75 cm apart, which could detect and record electromagnetic energy. The recordings were limited to frequencies below 30 Hz as man-made frequencies range from 50 Hz, 33.3 Hz and 25 Hz. Curiously, there were often huge 'kicks' of energy input being recorded that overloaded the equipment, which made the short duration recording totally unstable and extremely difficult to analyse. Was the joined serpent current's energy too great at this location? We decided to move to the southern portal stones where the Mary and Michael currents co-join and enter Avebury's stone circles. A 10-minute recording was made just north of the centre of the portal stones and some totally unexpected frequencies were recorded. The following graph is a spectrogram of the results, the dense vertical lines are the interfering man-made frequencies amidst general noise, but along the length of the spectrogram three faint and irregular horizontal lines can just be discerned, at about 24, 18 and 10 Hz.

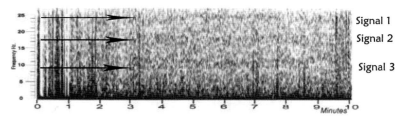

Electromagnetic readings of earth energy

These strange anomalous signals are the first solid recording of the electromagnetic frequency levels emitted by a dragon line. Rodney Hale is experienced in analysing electromagnetic data and has no explanation for them at present. At this location, the Mary line is about 6 metres (19.8 feet) wide and the three faint signals were taken from the first metre. We strongly suspect that there are other magnetic frequencies which lie across the earth current's width. Master dowsers, such as Dennis Wheatley and René de Bartiral, claim the Mary line comprises of 15 individual bands all of which resonate electromagnetic colour frequencies. Although further investigations are required to fully understand the magnetic characteristics of dragon lines, our initial results are very intriguing and we are currently involved in a long-term project to study energy lines with engineer David Webb.

Dowsers are convinced that they can detect invisible energies, underground water and minerals simply by using a dowsing instrument, but did ancient man use dowsing to locate earth energies? The simple art of dowsing is thousands of years old. In a French cave are Neolithic carvings of dowsing tools – referred to as *The Library of Dowsing*. The American dowser Sig Lonegren reported on cave art in Tassili, Algeria, in which a character holds a dowsing tool and is watched by onlookers. The art has been dated to 6000 BC. Dowsers are depicted on ancient Egyptian bas-reliefs and Cleopatra is reputed to have employed dowsers to find gold. Dowsers appear on a statue of the Chinese Emperor Kwang Su who reigned around 2200 BC. In the ancient world dowsing was considered a ritual art that located various substances or energies.

Archaeological dowsing

Dowsing has been used by several archaeologists to explore the ancient landscape. In the 1930s one of the pioneers of archaeological dowsing was Captain Boothby, who was a member of the British Society of Dowsers. Boothby investigated numerous prehistoric sites and noted that most Neolithic long barrows and Bronze Age round barrows were sited above underground streams. He was convinced this was a deliberate design feature.

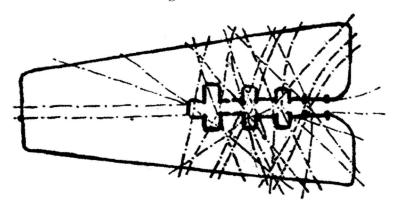

Survey of underground streams at Stoney Littleton long barrow, Wellow, Somerset by Guy Underwood

The streams set the axis of the mound and the width of the passageway

Intrigued by Boothby's findings, a renowned archaeologist, Reginald Allender Smith decided to investigate stone circles for any association with underground streams. Smith was a leading authority of the Stone Age, Keeper of the British and Roman Antiquities at the British Museum and Director of the Society of Antiquaries. Smith discovered that the presence of underground water at the exact centres of stone circles in the Wessex region was a significant design feature; he called this underground water source a 'blind spring'. A blind spring is where water is produced, chemically, deep within the earth, and under high pressure it is forced upwards through vertical fault lines and when the water reaches an impenetrable rock stratum it 'domes'. Every religion has a special use for water and to prehistoric people underground water consecrated the site.

The mysterious properties of underground water

Guy Underwood, a retired barrister and field archaeologist, (1883-1964) used dowsing in his archaeological investigations and he extended Smith's research. Using a highly sensitive dowsing instrument, he discovered that a blind spring naturally emits two distinctive patterns of electromagnetic energy - a spiral shape and a circular pattern.

Blind springs, sacred yin water

Blind springs are associated with primary water. To the mystic, primary water is alive, feminine, healing, and sacred. I call this water *yin water*, as it is produced chemically deep within the earth and it is completely independent of rainfall (yang water). Internally, the earth continually produces primary yin water and so a blind spring will never run dry. Pressure forces the yin water upwards through vertical fault lines and when it eventually reaches the surface, it is revered as a 'sacred spring'. Where it is bored defines a Holy Well. Ancient man used the geometric spiral energy pattern as a design canon for the positioning of stone circles and often erected standing stones above them. Underwood called the spiral pattern a 'geospiral' and persistent and careful dowsing revealed that a geospiral consists of magnetic coils that can manifest in multiples of 7 up to a maximum of 49. He noted that isolated standing stones, burial mounds and the central megalithic features of stone circles, such as the Obelisk at Avebury and the Altar Stone at Stonehenge were all set above a geospiral pattern. Underwood proposed that the geospiral motif inspired prehistoric artists to carve spiral patterns upon stones, ivory and other objects. To prehistoric people the spiral pattern has always been closely associated with water and the ceremonial way to approach a spiritual dimension. The geospiral pattern marks the esoteric centre of a site. For more information on this enigmatic and healing geodetic energy pattern read *Divining Ancient Sites – Insights into their creation* by Maria Wheatley.

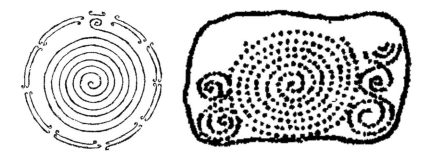

A geospiral pattern and a carved spiral motif

Interestingly, sacred trees of the Druid tradition, such as the yew, apple, hazel and hawthorn, which are well known for their healing or magical properties, invariably grow above a geospiral. The Druids were renowned for their in-depth understanding of Nature, and no doubt, these ancient masters fully understood the esoteric significance of the geospiral pattern and probably integrated it into their rituals and ceremonies. To the Aborigines of Australia a decorative spiral pattern, very similar to the geospiral motif, signifies a well or an underground water source and is deemed a sacred location.

When I was learning esoteric water divining I was taught that sacred healing springs and holy wells renowned for their medicinal properties are invariably sited above the geospiral pattern, indicating a prominent source of yin water. Yang water emits a distinctive pattern and an inharmonious energy field. Long-term exposure to this field is injurious to health, whereas, yin water emits a harmonic healing field. Both types of water are safe to drink.

Circular earth energy patterns

Underwood noted that a circular (or oval) pattern of surface energy always surrounded the geospiral pattern, which he called a primary halo. It consists of three concentric circles of magnetic energy and standing stones were always sited above it. The reason why the ancients chose a circular design for 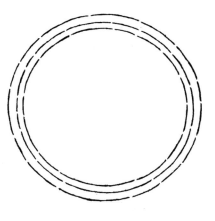 their stone circles and mounds, says Underwood, is due to the mysterious energy patterns the earth emits.

Further research revealed that exceptionally powerful blind springs generate six circles of energy. Stonehenge has six primary halo patterns and the ditch and bank, Aubrey holes and the Y and Z holes and the bluestone ring are all aligned above them. Guy Underwood produced the following survey in 1956 revealing how the ancient architects incorporated circular energy patterns into Stonehenge. It is widely known that underground water produces subtle changes in the earth's magnetic field and this is what causes the dowsing rod to react. The water does this because it generates a field of its own which interacts with the earth's magnetic field. Numerous professional water-diviners and dowsers have confirmed Smith and Underwood's work and it is highly plausible that our ancestors could detect the magnetic variations that the earth produces and revered its mysterious patterns.

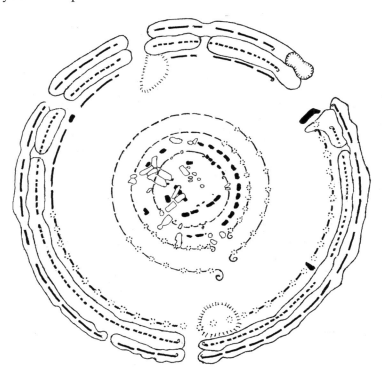

Stonehenge has six primary halo patterns

The earth's fault

Underwood also analysed other geological conditions at sacred sites and noted that several stone circles were associated with fault lines. The following survey of the Sanctuary, near Avebury shows the small fissure systems - geological fault lines - some of which are only four to six inches in width. The fissures appear to radiate from the centre of the stone circle and enclose the entire monument. Notice that the megaliths of the West Kennet Avenue, (located to the upper left of the survey) are also aligned between fault lines. Likewise, Stones 101-104 of Avebury's southern circle were positioned between narrow geological fault lines.

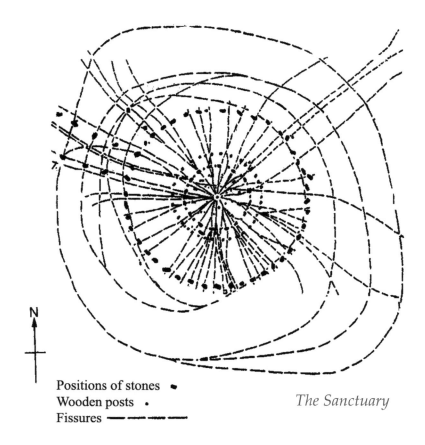

Positions of stones ·
Wooden posts ·
Fissures — ·· — ·· —

The Sanctuary

Fault lines and ancient sites

In the early 1980s geologist Paul McCartney studied the correlation between stone circles and fault lines. After investigating numerous ancient sites throughout England and Wales, he concluded that all stone circles are located within 1-2 miles of a fault line. The Mary and Michael dragon lines are also associated with geological fault lines and research twenty years ago established that fissures run all along the current's routes in Devon, Somerset, Wiltshire and Norfolk. Alfred Watkins also connected certain leys with fault lines. To my knowledge, the only ley to have been excavated was by Watkins in the 1920s. The topographical ley under investigation was linked to an old legend regarding an underground tunnel system in Herefordshire. When

Watkins dug into the line he found that it was a natural fault or long crevice and not man-made. Interestingly, megaliths that are erected near or above fault lines (and especially those sited on granite intrusions like the stone circles and stone rows of Dartmoor and Carnac in Brittany, France) are exposed to natural seismic-electrical surges. When pressure or movement occurs in the fault line the megaliths become bathed in a subtle form of electricity. Whilst the physical association between fault lines and earth-ley energy is recognised, the metaphysical implications still remain elusive.

Strange effects and shamanic visions in Greece

Dr Luigi Piccardi, a geologist who specialises in finding links between mythical descriptions and geological phenomena, suggests that the ancient Greeks deliberately sited sacred centres above active fault lines because these areas can produce spiritual visions. For example, the famous Oracle of Delphi in Greece was located upon a fault line where naturally occurring hallucinogenic vapours rise along the fissures from the hydrocarbon-bearing strata below. Piccardi suggests that most mythological sites in Greece are strongly correlated with active geological faults and veneration of these places may have been a result of people seeing unusual natural phenomena there. Earth mysteries expert, Paul Devereux, points out that 'earthlights', strange luminous balls of light, known to the ancient Celts as fairy lights are also associated with fault lines. The authors have seen this phenomenon in the Avebury region on numerous occasions.

Devereux documented an intriguing geological fact, which could explain why the ancients chose to site their stone circles above fault lines, and also align them to certain sunrises and sunsets. He points out that whenever the sun or moon crosses the horizon a *shear force* is exerted upon fault lines, which produces an energy flow upon the ground like a tidal pull. Therefore, at dawn and sunset subtle electromagnetic changes can take place which affect the megaliths. These findings cannot be coincidental and it seems reasonable to presume that the ancients would have constructed their megalithic temples in special locations where the power of the earth could be seen and felt.

The Dragon Project

The Dragon Project Trust was formed in the 1970s to analyse energetic anomalies at ancient sites. The founding directors were Paul Devereux and John Steel, and the team comprised scientists, electronic engineers, psychics and dowsers to investigate psychic archaeology, and to physically monitor the sites with scientific instruments  to measure levels of magnetic and radioactive radiations. One intriguing anomaly was noted in 1979 at the Rollright stone circle, Oxfordshire. Infrared photographs of the outlying King Stone showed an apparent hazy glow around the crest of the standing stone. Professional analysis of the photograph was unable to provide a logical explanation. In the following year another infrared photograph showed the image of a cloud formation hovering around 4.5 metres (15 feet) above the ground between the King Stone and the stone circle. Over prolonged periods of monitoring for other anomalies the researchers noted other curious phenomena which were recurring, such as sounds from the stones and the ground around them; soft but subtle light effects; strange happenings such as the malfunctioning of quartz wristwatches and alarm clocks used in the researches. Added to this was the bizarre behaviour of animals at the site such as their refusal to go near some megaliths at certain times whilst being quite content to be near them at other times.

Energy investigations at Avebury

The Dragon Project also found that levels of radioactivity within certain stone circles tend to be *lower* than the surrounding areas. As Avebury wasn't included in their primary studies, the authors and Rodney Hale conducted a series of tests to investigate the background ionising radiation levels at selected locations within the complex. Rodney was one of the original members of the Dragon Project and developed some of the instruments used in the researches. Using a recording Geiger counter we selected an area close to the Obelisk marker stone, which was monitored for 20 minutes, followed by 20 minutes at a point some 3 metres to the south. The readings were analysed by Rodney using the statistical 'T-test' to determine if there were any significant differences between the readings taken at the two locations. The expression 'significant' is commonly used when there is a probability of 95% or more that the difference really exists. However, no significant difference was detected at the Obelisk. The next location was a central position near the North West end of the West Kennet Stone Avenue, which was monitored for 18 minutes, followed by 18 minutes outside of the avenue. The mean count within the avenue was 68.3 and outside it was 70.1, which does not calculate any difference. It was looking doubtful whether Avebury had any radiation anomalies and so we decided to head for the Sanctuary on Overton Hill. The centre of the monument was chosen as it was sited above the crossing point of the Mary and Michael earth currents and numerous fissure systems radiate from the centre making the location a geodetic hotspot. It was monitored for 20 minutes, then 20 minutes outside of the site, and finally a further 15 minutes at the centre. When the readings were analysed by Rodney the results were startling as the levels of radiation were significantly *higher* at the centre than outside of the stone circle. Statistically there was a probability of about 98% that there was a real difference. Plotting the counts per minute at the Sanctuary showed an interesting effect seen clearly on the graph.

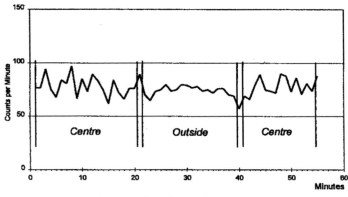

Radiation levels at the Sanctuary

Researchers have noted that natural radiation levels at ancient sites can produce strange and mysterious effects, such as flickering lights and even mirages have been reported. Mysterious lights are still being seen at the Sanctuary and one person told the authors that he saw *a small flickering light emerge from the centre of the monument, which darted around for a while before suddenly disappearing.*

Megalithic power – can you feel the force

We decided to investigate another energy phenomenon. According to the research of my late father when a standing stone is rooted into powerful earth energy lines or patterns, it will produce energy-bands known as *band transmissions*. Taller stones are said to have 5 bands above ground and two below making a total of 7 which equate to our chakras. Smaller stones have just 1-3. The stone absorbs the earth energy and transmits it in a laser-like beam of aerial electromagnetic ley-energy.

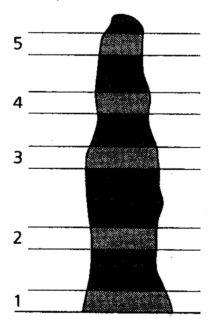

Band 2 transmits energy lines to local stones, such as those in a stone circle. Band 4 is associated with energy transmissions to distant stones or stone circles; connecting sacred site to sacred site across vast distances. I detect the bottom and tops of each band with a single L- rod by raising the rod slowly up the face of the stone. I wanted to prove to the academic world that these bands exist and Rodney Hale agreed to set a series of experiments to detect if they emitted a frequency.

Do they exist?

I located the bands using a dowsing rod. Rodney and Busty Taylor made a careful note of the bands positions. If the energy-bands really did produce electromagnetic energy then Rodney's equipment would detect and record the emitted frequency level. Rodney used a Wide-band (low Mhz) untuned radio receiver, a R.F. Spectrum Analyser and electronic equipment for recording any electromagnetic signals. Stone 101 in Avebury's southern circle was chosen for the first test, as it is one of the few stones that has not been re-erected and set in concrete.

Electromagnetic readings

For clarity in illustrating our results, the energy-bands on Stone 101 are shown as digitally produced coloured bands in the diagram on the following page. When the wide-band receiver was used the sound output from it (a general buzz or hiss) was recorded as the instrument was slowly and steadily raised from ground level to a height of 2 metres, which mirrored the dowsing technique. The signal strength has been plotted against the height of the stone for two separate tests and the width of the trace represents the strength of the signal. Notice that the electromagnetic signal correlates with the position of the energy bands. The strongest trace recorded was at Band 2, which is said to transmit energy to other standing stones, and if megaliths can pass on and receive this energy, one would expect this band to be the strongest. After analysing the data Rodney concludes that statistically there is a definite correlation between the energy bands and the recorded signal, and so this strongly suggests that the energy-bands really do exist and emit magnetic energy.

Feel the band's force

Band 3 produces a strange energy that can affect one's balance. Place the palms of the hand against it and lean at an angle of 45 degrees to the stone with your feet in tiptoe position. If you empty your mind of all thoughts, you will find that a force will push you either to the left or right. The direction of the force varies according to the lunar phases as it waxes and wanes, being at its strongest six days after the new or full moon.

Electromagnetic readings
Readings were taken at Avebury
by Rodney Hale

Macrochips

From Avebury to Silicon Valley in California megaliths and microchips share a common premise. All megaliths have a cubic crystal lattice construction; imagine a continuous set of small cubes interlinked through the entire stone and with atoms at the corners of each cube. This is identical to the modern-day semiconductor microchips grown in laboratories and which have revolutionised the electronics industry. Physicists have merely duplicated the stone's lattice structure; thus a megalith can be regarded as a semiconductor *macrochip* which theoretically has the capacity to store energy and information. But can a standing stone really transmit an aerial form of ley energy to other stones via Band 2 as we suggest?

Bob Sephton is a retired electrical engineer and experienced dowser. He wanted to detect the aerial ley energy that passes between standing stones and he experimented with different types of copper coils wired to an oscilloscope, an instrument for showing energy variations on a small screen. A coil based on the labyrinth in Chartres cathedral was placed at the end of a long pole and wired to the oscilloscope. He picked two standing stones, which he had dowsed for aerial ley energy. The idea of the long pole was to eliminate from the experiment any body radiations, which can sometimes be detected with electronic instruments.

The oscilloscope remained quiescent until Bob placed the coil within the energy line. The oscilloscope's horizontal line then danced wildly. On removing the coil the oscilloscope line sank back to the horizontal 'no energy' level. Bob's experiments have demonstrated that magnetic energy passes between standing stones which can be detected with either electronic equipment or dowsing rods. Perhaps the mysterious geophysical activity produced by the energy-bands and transmitted from megalith to megalith around and across the circumference of a stone circle was knowingly created and utilised by our distant ancestors.

The earth spirit

To ancient people the earth was sacred and was the mother of all things. Man appears to have believed that in the earth dwelt the 'soul substance' and that from the earth came the spirit which gives life to all things, and at death returned to it. There are many reasons for supposing that earth energies were regarded as a manifestation of this life spirit, which the prehistoric priesthood revered. The life force of the earth was known to numerous ancient societies, to the Sioux Nations of North America it was known as Wakonda and to the Australian Aborigines it was called Arungquiltha. The ancient Chinese referred to it as Chi and developed a geomantic science to explain it and ancient sites across the world stand as silent witnesses of long lost geodetic practises.

Chapter 3

Windmill hill solar temple

Long before Avebury's stone circles were raised our Neolithic ancestors constructed large megalithic structures, such as long barrows and circular or oval shaped earthen temples known as causewayed enclosures, and both were used as ceremonial centres. These are the oldest monuments in the ritual landscape predating the stone circle-building phase by over a thousand years. The Avebury area became a spiritual centre of global importance with over thirty long barrows and three large causewayed enclosures crowned the hilltops creating astronomical viewing arenas and sacred temple spaces.

Windmill Hill – the light of the sun

Windmill Hill is situated 1 mile (1.6 km) north west of Avebury and contains one of the largest causewayed enclosures in Europe. In the 18th century William Stukeley visited the site and recognised its antiquity. So velvety soft was the grass beneath his feet and so sweet was the air scented with the aroma of wild flowers that Stukeley thought the site magnificent. However, it wasn't until archaeological excavations in the 20th century that its Neolithic date was firmly established. Around 5500 years ago, (orthodox dating) three concentric rings of segmented banks and ditches were constructed upon the hilltop. Personifying a protective spiritual circle the enclosure was a ceremonial centre for the surrounding communities. Aligned upon the highly energized primary halo pattern which was described earlier, Windmill Hill was the earliest solar observatory and temple in the Avebury environs. Like other prehistoric monuments, the causewayed enclosure was developed in several stages, which began with the construction of the innermost circle of earthworks and the ditch formed an oval shaped entrance. At a later date, the middle circuit of small banks was erected, although oddly they began to collapse soon after their construction and no attempt was made to repair them. Standing upon this energy circle may hold the answer. Beneath your feet a ripple-effect of energy can be felt or dowsed which is stronger than other haloes and a sudden energy surge may have destabilised the banks. Earth energy 'quakes' are exceptionally rare and geologists dismiss their existence. Yet many leys and the Mary and Michael currents in part of their courses are intimately associated with fault lines.

Finally, the monumental outer circuit was built with its distinctive earthen banks standing around 1½-2 metres high (4-6 feet). Today, only the earthworks and the outer ditch in the eastern sector have survived as much of the monument was destroyed by ploughing. When viewed from the north the remnants of the causewayed enclosure can still be seen as distinctive 'parchmarks' - ghostly outlines that encircle the hillside reminding us of the glory that was.

The reason why the segmented earthworks were constructed has baffled archaeologists for years because they do not appear to have a practical function. Since the 1930s a wide range of interpretations have been mooted from cattle kraals, seasonal settlement camps, trade centres to defensive structures. During our research and interaction with the energies of Windmill Hill we discovered the reason why the causeways were created, we have seen their splendour and invite you to witness their original design.

Capturing the sun

We read earlier that solar alignments were skilfully integrated into Avebury's megalithic architecture and the passing of the seasons was celebrated at the key points of the ritual year.

Windmill Hill's earthen temple was the precursor of Avebury's megalithic sundial and its ceremonial design was to visually define the solstices and equinoxes. Ingeniously landscaped, the segmented earthworks in the eastern sector of the outer circuit acted like a time-marker. At the Quarter Days (solstices and equinoxes) as the rising sun appeared over the horizon it was perfectly framed by the causeways. Year after year, the causeways captured and embraced the sun and you can still see vestiges of this poetic alignment today, as the movements of the sun have scarcely changed in the past 5000 years. The main causeway entrance was clearly aligned to face the equinox sunrise which captures the sun's luminous rays as it rises on the far horizon.

Windmill Hill's causewayed enclosure predates the Avebury stone circles by a thousand years. Standing upon the hill you can see Silbury Hill in the distance and the West Kennet long barrow. Now turn around 180 degrees and count 3 fields in the distance. You would have seen a large concentric stone circle that was sadly smashed up in the 1800s.

Unfortunately, we cannot appreciate the full geomantic symmetry of the alignments as the earthen banks have eroded and now appear as mere bumps on the ground. The photograph on the following page shows a tentative reconstruction of a small section of the earthen temple, which shows a projected, although not exact, height of the segmented bank that once framed the sun's orb. With ideal weather conditions the rising sun would have appeared much lower on the horizon resting on the distant hill range and aligning with the causeway gap. On this particular Beltane (May Day) the clouds obscured the moment of sunrise and so the sun appears much higher in the sky.

The equinox sunrise. The sun aligns with the eastern causeway

Mists often rise to greet you at the equinox

Windmill Hill's causewayed enclosure 5500 years ago. The banks mirror the horizon and the causeway aligns with the sunrise

Horizon calendars

Another example of a landscape calendar was created by the Hopi Indian culture. Using the land's topography the Hopi culture created a horizon-based calendar. The position of the sun relative to certain contours and niches in the hills gave the precise time of the year for agricultural and ceremonial purposes. Metaphysically, this is an alchemic marriage of the sun (male) to the earth (female). Undoubtedly, the

Hopi landscape was sculptured so that the sun would rise perfectly in the gaps as it does on Windmill Hill.

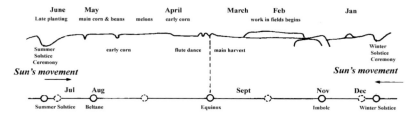

The Hopi culture horizon calendar

Earth power

Interestingly, the location within Windmill Hill's earthen temple which permits an unrestricted view of the solar alignments is a geodetic hot spot. The area was divined by the Neolithic priesthood and chosen as a ritualistic viewing area, as the Mary and Michael dragon lines and a powerful 21-coiled geospiral mark the site. Furthermore, the skilful fusion of celestial alignments and earth energies united the heavens with the earth's internal energy system.

Sacred location

Around one and a half thousand years later the Bronze Age astronomer-priests reused the enclosure and several burial mounds were placed upon and around its summit. The largest and most impressive round barrow was sited above the geodetic power spot, echoing the burial practises of the ancient Chinese geomants who located the crossing points of the all-powerful dragon lines for the sites of temples or the tombs of their emperors.

Spiritual topography, locating the planet's life force manifesting as energy lines or patterns, is one of the outstanding geodetic traditions of the old pagan religion. The round and feminine shaped bowl barrow sited upon the summit of the enclosure was aligned to face the midsummer sunrise, which we captured in the following photograph.

The midsummer sunrise
At the Summer Solstice the sun rises in its extreme north
east position and for 3-4 days it rises in the same spot - at its
standstill or solstice. With clear skies the sun appears to 'sit',
momentarily, on the nearby hill range.

Secrets of the barrows

There is another design canon that has been overlooked which we discovered. Annually, at every midwinter sunset the shadow cast by the large bell barrow courses across the ceremonial landscape, climbs upon and touches the nearby bowl barrow as if gently arousing the occupants from their ancestral slumber. Likewise, at the midsummer sunrise the shadow of the bowl barrow unites and engulfs the bell barrow. Go to Windmill Hill and see the barrow's shadow effect which was designed by our ancestors long gone. Unlike the nearby megalithic long barrows which were aligned to various sunrise events, Windmill Hill's round mounds and the standing stones of Avebury's southern inner circle incorporated the sun's light which produces dark shadow-lines to cast meaning upon their lives. Yin and yang, winter and summer, day and night, the sun and the shadow created unity and a sense of wholeness within the landscape.

The sun and the shadow
The large bell barrow was orientated to the midwinter sunset and the midsummer sunrise and its shadow-line touches and aligns with the nearby bowl barrow.

Windmill Hill, near Avebury predates Avebury's stone circles by one thousand years. It consisted of three oval segmented earthworks creating a ceremonial temple space. Sections of the eastern sector have survived but only the ghostly 'parchmarks' of the central and middle ditches can be seen.

Thornborough Henges, stars in the land

Constructed around the same time as Windmill Hill's causewayed enclosure, the triple henges of Thornborough in North Yorkshire are magnificent. The three almost identical and equally spaced henge monuments are each placed approximately 550 metres (1805 feet) apart and the alignment extends for nearly 1.7 km (1 mile). The central henge is positioned on the site of an older Cursus monument that was over a 1 km (quarter of a mile) in length and aligned to the midsummer sunrise.

Dr. Jan Harding discovered that certain celestial alignments were integrated into the site. The henge's share the same astronomical alignment as the pyramids at Giza in Egypt and are aligned to Orion's Belt - the three distinct stars in the constellation of Orion the Hunter. According to archaeologists, the site was first used around 3500 BC (orthodox dating) and it continued to be a ritual centre drawing pilgrims from across the North, at least until 2600 BC (orthodox dating). Dr Harding says the henge's are a mirror image of Orion in its highest position with the southern entrances framing the bright star Sirius as it appeared over the horizon. We saw the sun's orb being perfectly framed by the segmented banks at Windmill Hill and at Thornborough the earthen banks were likewise landscaped to frame a celestial object. These recent discoveries prove that the Neolithic priesthood in Britain were adept astronomers skilful at integrating solar and stella alignments into their earthen temples one thousand years before the Giza pyramids were constructed. Britain's esoteric priesthood brought heaven to earth and monumentalized the landscape creating celestial fusion of earth and sky, man and cosmos.

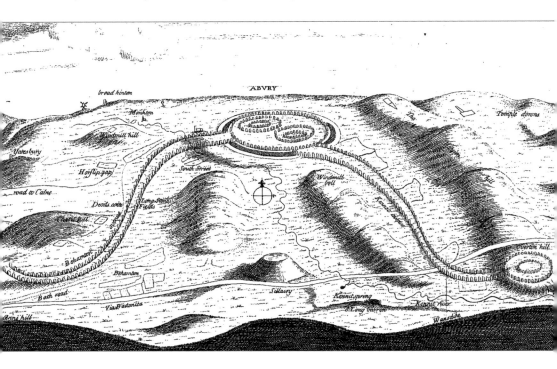

Chapter 4

Silbury, the Sanctuary & the end of an era

A vebury Henge was an extraordinary Neolithic temple of awesome proportions and breathtaking symmetry. Set in the ritual landscape this colossal construction was without parallel in prehistoric Europe and it emerged as a Neolithic world wonder. Never before in history had such a megalithic project been attempted, and generation after generation worked to complete the stone temple which took over one thousand years. Around 3000 BC (orthodox dating) the Obelisk and the Cove Stones were raised above an energetic spiral pattern and a small ditch and bank enclosed an area that designated sacred space. In c2800 BC (orthodox dating) 60 large sarsens were selected from Fyfield

Down and the northern and southern inner circles were constructed. Their location, shape and size were determined by a circular band of electromagnetic energy which gave the megaliths geophysical power. Approximately two hundred years later the henge bank was heightened and the gigantic outer circle was built, which was followed by the monumental construction of the meandering stone avenues. Following the Michael earth energy current the 2.41 km (1.5 mile) long West Kennet Avenue led to a small stone circle known as the Sanctuary on Overton Hill. In 1723 William Stukeley witnessed the destruction of the Sanctuary by a local farmer. The stones were only around 1.5 metres (4-5 feet) high and easily dragged away and the site was lost until Maud Cunnington rediscovered it in 1930. Stukeley called the circle *The Temple of the Earth* and thought it was dedicated to the earth mother. We read earlier that the Sanctuary is a geodetic hotspot with unusual radiation levels and the authors believe that this was once Avebury's energetic power centre.

Stukeley's drawing of the Sanctuary on Overton Hill

Silbury Hill
The moat surrounding Silbury Hill can fill with water
revealing a perfect reflection of the mound. Orginally, the
moat would have contained water all year round.

Silbury Hill

Located only a half mile south of the Henge and cradled by the West Kennet and Beckhampton stone avenues Silbury Hill was sited at the heart of the Avebury complex. Rising 40 metres (130 feet) from the valley floor and occupying over five and a half acres at its base, Silbury was the largest prehistoric mound in Neolithic Europe. However, Silbury Hill is only half of the monument as a substantial moat surrounds the mound and during the winter months the deeply cut ditch fills with water. Maud Cunnington pointed out that without the silt deposits; the ditch would be full of water all the year round. Silbury's presence in the landscape is unmistakeable and it was an important component in Avebury's grandiose design.

Silbury's lost avenue

Whilst surveying Avebury in the late 1950s Guy Underwood investigated the area surrounding Silbury Hill and claims that he saw the vestiges of an earthen avenue that led to Avebury. It ran from Silbury due north east, crossed the Winterbourne river and coursed across Waden Hill and entered Avebury in the south west sector. Silbury's lost avenue has yet to be confirmed by archaeologists, but it seems plausible that a processional way would have been constructed which linked Silbury to the Henge. Silbury's location was chosen as the Mary current flows through the mound. The lost avenue follows part of Mary's meandering course and then it follows geodetic energy lines that flow towards Avebury Henge.

The Avebury complex was a magnificent religious power centre which straddled the Wiltshire downs for 4.8 km (3 miles) and attracted pilgrims from far and wide. But despite its elaborate and sophisticated design around 1000 BC (orthodox dating) the site was abandoned. Why?

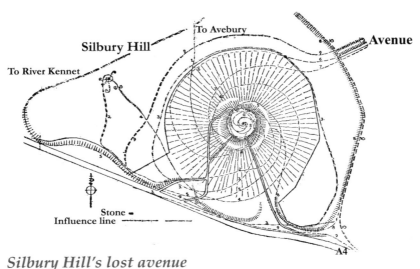

To Avebury

Silbury Hill

Avenue

To River Kennet

Stone ■
Influence line

A4

Silbury Hill's lost avenue
Notice the geospiral creates a vortex - its energy flows forming and dictating the avenue's position

Across Northern Europe the Neolithic people constructed numerous megalithic sites and if their stone temples were used for rituals and supplications in the ancient religions then high on the spiritual agenda of the New Stone Age people would be the fertility of the land and idyllic weather conditions for their crops. In the Neolithic period Northern Europe basked in the warmth and blue skies of the prevailing Sub-Boreal climate which was ideal for crop growing. Year after year the gods had heeded their prayers and had provided them with a superb environment and were man's strongest allies. Today's harvest rituals may have originated in the men and women of prehistory giving thanks to the gods for such bountiful harvests under perfect climatic conditions. The warm Sub-Boreal climate continued through the Early Bronze Age and the megalithic building programme across Northern Europe flourished. However, around 1500 BC (orthodox dating) the European circle programme appears to have come to a somewhat abrupt end. Was the cessation of the programme due to a major cultural change with the arrival of the age of metallurgy? Certainly, there were some dramatic changes in funerary customs, for example. The Neolithic ethos built long barrows in which to inter the multiple bones of clan or family members. With the Bronze Age came the funerary custom of single inhumations with grave goods, under round barrows with the accent on individualism. The New Stone Age farming industry was now complemented with the metal industry producing a wide variety of artefacts, so there was a change in tools and weapons but farming remained the largest industry across Europe. Strangely, our forebears faced exactly what we are facing today - climatic change.

The ending of the megalithic building era was not, according to climatic experts, due to a cultural change but a climatic change. The idyllic Sub-Boreal climate gave way to the Sub-Atlantic weather of grey skies, rain and high winds. Supplication to the gods for the ideal Sub-Boreal conditions would, no doubt, have increased in intensity but, year after year, the colder and harsher Sub-Atlantic conditions prevailed. No amount of rituals or offerings bought an end to the dismal weather patterns, whose advent must have been catastrophic to the New Stone Age people. There was probably a gradual movement from the colder, high grounds and the windswept scarps such as Salisbury Plain to the lower lands elsewhere, more conducive to crop growth. The stone circles were abandoned, and lashed with the Sub-Atlantic gales and rains, gathered mosses and lichens being no longer maintained by the clan members. An era had simply ended. *We face their plight and should heed climatic change.*

On the other hand, did the earth and megalithic energy system with its laser-like energy beams that transverse the landscape somehow overload causing some of the megaliths to topple? We are currently investigating the latter as clues prevail. Coupled with climatic change this scenario would have been devastating. Stone circles overloaded with intense energy may have been temporarily regarded as no go areas.

Esoteric traditions kept alive

Despite religious, climatic and cultural changes, the knowledge of harnessing the subterranean energies into the foundation plans of megalithic temples was handed down through the Bronze and Iron Ages to the Medieval Masonic brotherhood. This was a closely guarded secret kept from the church hierarchy who would have turned on the masons with vengeance had they known that the Christian churches were being constructed to pagan design canons.

During his archaeological investigations of medieval structures, Underwood discovered that circular and spiral earth energy patterns were carefully integrated into Christian churches and cathedrals that mirrored the geomantic design features of the megalithic builders. For instance, Salisbury cathedral is sited above a circular energy pattern, and its spire, the tallest and most impressive in England, stands over its centre. Salisbury cathedral is by no means unique in this respect.

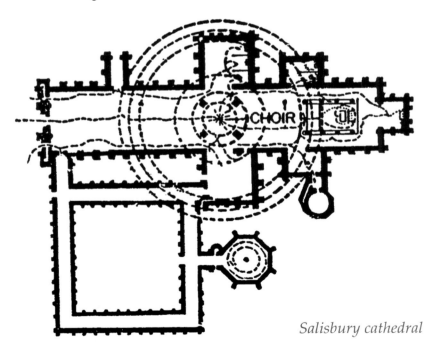

Salisbury cathedral

The Knights Templar, likewise, set the foundation plans of their churches in line with geodetic energies. Whilst tracking the yin and yang dragon lines, the late Hamish Miller and Gary Biltcliffe noted that the serpentine energy currents often set the axis of medieval Christian constructs. Many other churches were positioned upon sites of previous antiquity, or placed upon an ancient linear line, and thus continuing the pagan tradition of locating religious sites upon ley lines.

At sacred sites such as Avebury and Stonehenge, which are the equivalents to megalithic cathedrals, we can sense that each site has its own distinctive 'persona' or 'spirit of place' each totally unique. Likewise, churches and cathedrals all exude a different 'spirit of place'. This is because they have all been carefully integrated with the prevailing earth energies at their locations. The energies imbue the constructs with a sense of harmonious balance. Earth and ley energy associated with ancient sites is not acceptable to the scientific establishment. Yet, alongside Rodney Hale, our investigations revealed that a form of megalithic energy exists and electromagnetic frequencies are closely associated with dragon lines and high radiation levels are present within the centre of the Sanctuary. Over a period of one year, the experiments concerning megalithic ley energy and radiation levels at the Sanctuary were repeated several times. Each individual test produced the same results and data, thus meeting the criteria required by the scientific community that insists one must be able to measure or weigh and to replicate results in experiments. Earth and ley energy can no longer be easily dismissed as flights of fancy created by over-imaginative dowsers and there are too many coincidences here to reject our work.

Undeniably, divining the land and harnessing its invisible energy was essential to the geomancers who constructed ancient sites. The megalithic architecture was closely determined by the geophysical energies creating regional power centres of which the Avebury Henge temple was the most profound, spiritual statement in stone and earth.

The Cove Stones and the Obelisk Stone were selected for astronomical alignments, and the movement of celestial bodies, the megaliths rooted into magnetic earth currents; and the key moments in the annual cycle of the earth's rotation could be made to combine and to generate an energy whose force is still dimly active today. This geomantic formula undoubtedly produced para-terrestrial events, such as flickering lights, spiritual visions and apparitions that were considered an integral part of the Old Religion. Avebury was, and will always be, a truly magical place.

The Avebury School of Esoteric Studies Professional Certificated courses

Affiliated with the *Association of British Correspondence Colleges* offering practical workshops, on-line lessons/webiners, personal SKYPE lessons, CD-Rom home study packages or traditional hardback manual courses.

The dowsing courses: *Professional Dowsing* and the *Master Practitioner of Dowsing* are not taught anywhere else in the world and they are the result of over 70 years of combined research. Expert tuition alongside practical exercises will give you a deep understanding of the ancient art of dowsing using dowsing instruments *and* your body.

Certificated Dowsing Courses

Dowsing professionally
Explores dowsing in detail so that the beginner, or any dowsing student, can easily grasp how to dowse for a variety of different things from powerful earth energies to the chakra and aura system; making this the foremost dowsing course in the UK. ***Making learning simple*** with practical and visual learning tools, Maria offers videos of how to dowse, so that you can see how a particular dowsing task can be achieved.

Professional Dowsing Advanced level
Master Practitioner certificated course
Divining the Earth – Harmonic Living The UKs most highly developed dowsing course on earth energies, leys, sacred water, geodetic energies and grid lines. Study this course in two practical workshops, or with a home study package, on line, or SKYPE lessons. After studying this course you will become a **Master Practitioner of Dowsing** with exceptional ability to attune to the Earth Force and interpret its invisible flows and frequencies.

The course has two sections.

- *Level I Geodetic earth energies and ley lines.*
- *Level II The Healing and Shadow Grid Lines.*

Maria is often invited to teach overseas and welcomes any enquires. She also leads dowsing tours of sacred sites in the UK, Scotland, Ireland and Europe.

For more information:
www.theaveburyexperience.co.uk
mariawheatley@aol.com   01672 511427